A *Band* *of* Bears

THE RAMBLING LIFE OF A LOVABLE LONER

BY JONI PHELPS HUNT

LONDON TOWN PRESS

Jean-Michel Cousteau *presents*

Publishing Director
Jean-Michel Cousteau

Series Editor
Vicki León

A Band of Bears

Principal photographer
Jeff Foott

Additional photographers
Tom Bean; John Cancalosi; J.M. Labat/Jacana; Wayne Lankinen;
Wayne Lynch; Tom McHugh; Mark D. Phillips; Art Wolfe

London Town Press
P.O. Box 585
Montrose, California 91021
www.LondonTownPress.com

Book design by Christy Hale
10 9 8 7 6 5 4 3 2 1

Printed in Singapore

Distributed by Publishers Group West

Library of Congress Cataloging-in-Publication Data
Hunt, Joni Phelps
A band of bears : the rambling life of a lovable loner / by
Joni Phelps Hunt.
p. cm.—(Jean-Michel Cousteau presents)
Includes index.
ISBN-13: 978-0-9766134-5-9 (softcover)
ISBN-10: 0-9766134-5-X (softcover)
1. Bears—Juvenile literature. I. Title.
QL737.C27H85 2006
599.78—dc22
                                        2006027970

FRONT COVER: An Alaskan brown bear cub looks like the world's
favorite stuffed animal. Teddy bears got their name from Teddy
Roosevelt, who as U.S. President once refused to shoot a live bear.

TITLE PAGE: It may look like a nap to us but more likely the
polar bear patiently waits to ambush a seal about to come up
for air at a breathing hole in the ice. A polar's powerful nose can
easily smell a faraway seal or whiff rotting meat 20 miles away.

BACK COVER: Polar bears, except for females with cubs, go
through life alone. Sometimes, though, two adults will pair up
to play. Polar bears have smaller heads than other bears, letting
them get through holes in the ice to catch seals.

Contents

▲ A well-fed grizzly is a bear that naps. The half-eaten salmon it leaves doesn't go to waste. Younger bears, females with cubs, and seagulls sneak up to eat the leftovers from older bears.

Bears appeal to us, partly because they have qualities we think of as human. They're highly curious. They give bear hugs. They bounce to their feet and stand upright. They spend time sitting on their fat rumps.

And they love to eat; some have a sweeter tooth than we do. Although the giant panda prefers bamboo and the polar bear goes for seal blubber, the other six species of bruin will eat almost anything and go almost anywhere to get it. Bears devour salmon and fawns, berries and rodents, clams and skunk

cabbage. Bears also sip nectar from bird feeders, fight over dead moose carcasses, and dig for ground squirrels. In summer, these animals even gorge themselves on moths! (On a good day, a bear can down 40,000 of those babies.)

These intelligent mammals have many sides to their personalities. Most are lifelong loners. On the other hand, bear mothers are devoted single moms and ferocious parents. They need to be, since some male bears make a habit of killing cubs.

Sometimes cranky or just plain aggressive,

there's a Pooh Bear side to these powerful animals. Park rangers and naturalists have countless stories. On one occasion, a ranger spotted an inquisitive bear and gave it a blast of pepper spray to shoo it away from campers. His aim wasn't perfect, however—and he found himself in a stinging cloud of spray. Eyes burning, the ranger ran for the nearest creek and started rinsing his face. Suddenly he heard campers laughing. The ranger looked up to see the bear he had sprayed squatting right beside him, washing its own face and looking over at him from time to time.

A polar bear has black skin but most of it is covered with fur. Only its nose, mouth, and pads on the paws show. This helps the bear sneak up on wary prey with big eyes, like seals.

Bears got their start when a small bearlike dog began to evolve; five million years ago, its descendants became the Ursidae, the bear family. Spreading across the world, bears populated all continents except Antarctica and Australia. (Australian koalas are marsupials, not bears.)

Like their dog ancestors, bears had good-sized canines and incisors. These meat-eaters also grew molars, enlarging their diets to include a variety of plants. This made bears into omnivores, like human beings.

A bear is built to forage efficiently. Its deft paws can lift logs, strip berries from a branch, or hook a salmon from the water.

Strong shoulders and short but muscular legs allow the bear to dig fast. Big five-toed feet help it stand tall or run on all fours to capture prey. A zoo animal might look slow and clumsy, but a wild bear steps lively. Some species really gallop on those stubby legs, reaching up to 40 miles an hour in bursts.

Over time, bear claws got more specialized. Polar claws became thick and razor-sharp. Black bears developed curved claws, excellent for tree-climbing. The claws of grizzlies got longer and straighter, letting them dig out dens or ground squirrels with ease.

Species vary in size but all have strong

▼ The mouth of a bear has 42 teeth—and some of them are long, sharp, and scary-looking. They are called "canines," a word that comes from the scientific name for the dog family.

▲ The front paws of a polar bear are bigger than a dinner plate—up to a foot across. Partly webbed, the paws act as paddles in the icy Arctic water. Paws are padded with fur for extra warmth.

stocky bodies. The 100-pound sun bear stands four feet high on its hind legs. It is dwarfed by the polar bear, which at up to 2,000 pounds, stands a terrifying ten feet tall.

Good insulation from thick fur allows bears to live in hot and cold climates. They thrive in ecosystems from the pack ice and tundra of the Arctic Circle to the barren edge of Asia's Gobi desert. They wander the shrinking bamboo forests of China and the urban woodlands of Pennsylvania. Bears prowl the mountain wilds of South America, the humid rainforests of India, the crowded urban islands of Japan, and the uncrowded islands of the Bering Sea.

▲ To polar bears, this huge harsh world is home. But threats to their survival loom. As temperatures on earth rise and the Arctic ice melts sooner, polars have fewer places to hunt seals—and less time to build much-needed layers of blubber. The danger of pollution from oil drilling and tanker spills also grows. Oil and other chemicals harm polar bears, since they lick their fur to groom themselves.

◄ An important source of fatty food for North American bears is salmon. Each year, in runs such as this one at Adams River in British Columbia, two species of bears gather to fish and feast on several species of salmon.

◄ When there are plenty of salmon, black bears and grizzlies eat the fatty parts first—the skin and eggs. The fat on this dog salmon will help the grizzly put on weight to live through its next hibernation.

A big swath of Alaska and Canada contains the largest concentration of bears. It's the only place in the world where three species are found in abundance.

These furry hunters and gatherers have well-developed senses. Although their eyes look as small as raisins in those huge Yogi Bear heads, most species see well and have good night vision. Some species also see in color, useful to spot fruit as it ripens.

Their sense of touch is precise, thanks to sensitive paws that can manipulate objects and pick up tiny, fast-moving items, such as tasty ants. (Like human beings with potato chips, bears can't stop with just one.)

Large ears and acute hearing let them detect sounds better than human beings. But a bear really excels in the nose department. Inside its mouth, specialized nerve endings enhance its sniffer. By opening its mouth and "drinking" air, it inhales smells. Bears use scent to avoid each other—and to meet for mating. Upwind they can catch the aroma of food, rotting meat, or a human being miles away.

◄ Adult bears wade in to grab salmon in their jaws. Sometimes they stand on shore and hook fish with their claws. Other times, they go into deep water. Bears can open their eyes underwater but they try to keep their ears dry.

An eat-anything forager

*I*n the wilderness, bears roam in tune with the seasons. As they awaken from hibernation, they forage on spring plants. Alaskans often see bears along roadsides and shorelines, munching green shoots.

For bears lean and ravenous from their winter's nap, summer is calorie-loading time. They eat gross amounts of ripening fruit, salmon, mushrooms, mammals, and anything else they can get their paws on. One researcher saw a black bear crack and eat 2,605 hazelnuts in one day. Another biologist watched a bear consume over 25,000 tent caterpillars at one marathon feeding session!

◄At McNeil River, Alaskan coastal bears come together to fish for their most important food. Bears are usually skittish around each other. During these salmon runs, a few bears fight, standing to do battle. But most bears ignore each other so all can benefit. The river becomes wall-to-wall bears. The best fishing sites, below the falls, go to the biggest, most dominant animals.

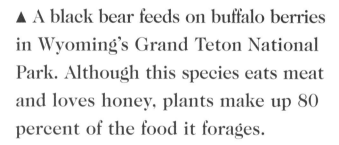

▲ A black bear feeds on buffalo berries in Wyoming's Grand Teton National Park. Although this species eats meat and loves honey, plants make up 80 percent of the food it forages.

Insects furnish surprising amounts of fatty energy. To bears, fat-rich foods are more important than protein. A bear in luck may catch 15 salmon a day and will eat the fatty brains, skin, and eggs first.

Bears have a short window of time to gain weight. In order to survive the next hibernation, grizzlies may gulp down 20,000 calories a day to build six to ten inches of fat. Black bears put on 30 pounds a week. Female bears gain four times their body fat to get through pregnancy and have enough milk for their cubs.

We tend to think only of winter as hibernation time, but some bears spend up to seven months snoozing away! Species living in mild climates, however, don't hibernate at all.

The polar bear is different. To give birth and care for young, female polars make dens. Males do not make dens or hibernate. They can, however, slow down their body functions

if they fail to find prey for two weeks. In this state, called "walking hibernation," the animals live on stored fat and do not drink or urinate.

Bears have home ranges, though they seldom defend them. Moving between higher and lower elevations, they follow the flowering of plants, the seasons for nuts and berries, and the migrations of prey animals like caribou.

As they travel, bears stick to the familiar.

▲ Most bear species need lots of room to roam. A wide-open place like Shoshone National Forest provides home ranges for many grizzlies. A grizzly travels all around its range to find a mate, locate drinking water, and hunt food, from ripening berries to salmon.

Biologists have discovered that bears regularly follow networks of trails, well worn from thousands of bearprints. Bears often walk exactly where the paws of their forebears once stepped.

Most of the time, they take pains to avoid other bears. When salmon spawn or blackberries get ripe, however, seasonal feasts bring bears together. To avoid battles, bears organize themselves into dominance hierarchies—a fancy name for a bear version of the pecking order.

To feed without feuding, bears ignore each other, a tactic called avoidance behavior. When a subadult or younger bear arrives at Alaska's McNeil River during the salmon run, it ignores the bears already fishing. They appear to ignore the newcomer also. Nevertheless, each bear's posture and behavior sends a message about its status.

◄ Every day is lesson time for grizzly cubs. Here, two of them mimic the fishing moves that their mother makes. The blood-stained muzzles of both cubs show that they've already sampled. One still has a salmon tidbit to finish.

Lower-ranking animals like subadults and females without cubs do not look directly at other bears. Staring, a challenge gesture, could lead to conflict. Low-ranking bears wait for the dominant bears to get their fill, and never ever try to take the best fishing spots.

The home range of a male bear may overlap with that of other males and several females. In the Canadian Yukon, the home range for a male brown bear is about 250 square miles. In the Brooks Range, an Alaskan male grizzly occupies 520 square miles, a female grizzly one-quarter as much. Black bears occupy more compact ranges, from ten to 52 square miles.

Because of habitat destruction, China's giant panda must make do with very little. A panda in Wolong Reserve has roughly one to three square miles of home range, which it shares with other pandas.

Ursus behavior from birth to denning

◄ A young black bear cub investigates the world outside its den. When it's born, it's blind and the size of an orange. By two months, the cub's eyes are open, its fur thickens, and it's eager to explore.

The name "Curious George" fits the average bear as well as it does a monkey. Aware bears can't help snooping and sniffing, their curiosity led by their high-powered noses.

Since bears prefer to live alone, they communicate long-distance to keep from running into each other. How? Through a smell-based system of marking.

Researchers once thought that bears scratched where it itched by rubbing up against any old tree. But marking trees, often growing near well-used trails, are like bruin newspapers. A bear rips off bark, claws the tree until sap runs, then rubs itself against it, leaving hairs. Bears leave their signs on telephone poles and other manmade structures, too.

Scent markings help to keep two bear species safely apart within the same home range. If black bears and grizzlies bump into each other by accident, the black bear would get the worst of it. In all likelihood, it would be injured or killed.

Using the spray and sniff method, bears also mark home ranges with urine. Most messages say "Stay away!" But some mean "I'm looking for a mate." The scent left by a hopeful male bear can cause females to come into heat. Females leave scent signals, too. A hormone in their urine tells male bears that they are ready for courtship.

Black and grizzly bears breed May to September, polar bears somewhat earlier. Males may fight or bluff charge at each other over females. Once partners are sorted out, they pair off to nuzzle, wrestle, and mate. Both males and females may mate with more than one partner during the two-week breeding season.

The female can delay the development of her fertilized eggs for up to five months after mating. She does so to make sure her cubs will be born in the safe warmth of a den.

When she's not busy eating for two or more, a pregnant female makes a large den, adding grasses for extra snugness. Existing dens, especially if dry and hidden, are often reused. She makes new dens in caves, hollow trees, or under rocks and tree roots. It may take her a week to dig the tunnel and egg-shaped sleeping area. Pregnant bears and those with first-year cubs enter dens earlier, usually mid-September, and leave them later.

▲ Bears build dens under rocks and tree roots and on steep slopes. Snowdrifts give good insulation, keeping dens warmer. Female bears prepare larger dens since they give birth to cubs during hibernation.

Male black bears and grizzlies retreat to smaller dens to avoid winter weather and food shortages. Unlike other hibernating animals, bears can be awakened, letting them react quickly to danger. This also allows females to care for cubs born during hibernation.

How can such a big animal hibernate for two to seven months without food or water? While denning, it can adapt its breathing and heart rate to drop by more than half. In hibernation, it burns up a quarter of its weight at about 4,000 calories per day.

The pregnancy of a healthy female bear only takes about two months, slightly

▶Grizzly cubs wrestle and growl at each other, play fighting on the McNeil River in Alaska. In real battles, bears show their teeth and hit hard. Cubs also play tag with their brothers or sisters. To turn somersaults, they hold onto their feet and roll.

longer for polar bear females. Cubs are tiny compared to moms. A 450-pound brown bear produces a squirrel-sized cub. Polar cubs are somewhat chubbier. A newborn panda would fit in a teacup.

Born singly or up to five in a litter, cubs are born blind, with sparse hair. To find mother's milk, they use long sharp claws to pull through her fur. Lying on her side, the bear mother cradles them with her warmth, nursing cubs with milk as rich as whipped cream. Cubs feed often, humming loudly. At two months, their eyes open and their fur thickens. But the family stays in the den until the weather gets mild and food is available.

Once out in the world, cubs follow their mother, their teacher. Watching her, they learn to fish, forage for plants, dig roots, and return to favorite berrybushes, beehives, and ant colonies. At times a black bear mother goes off to forage, first parking her cubs beneath a big tree so that they can scurry up at any sign of danger.

The greatest danger comes from male bears. If a male threatens her cubs, the mother bear charges—or flees elsewhere with her young. In spite of her care, her offspring may lose their lives to other

◄ Cubs nurse frequently in their first months. When a female bear senses there are no threats in the area, she may nurse her cubs sitting—or even lying on her back. She may have up to five babies, but litters of two or three are most common.

▲ Even as older cubs, polar bears get up to mischief. In mock fights, they nip and slap. They lunge at each other, attempting a polar bear hug or faking a bite. They try new wrestling holds and foot kicks. For fun, older cubs also grab onto small icebergs in the water and rock them, knocking off their bear playmates.

predators like coyotes, or to storms, accidents, forest fires, and disease. As many as half of all cubs do not live to celebrate their first birthday.

Human hunters have horror stories about tangling with mother bears. A deer hunter in southwest Washington got chased up a pine by an irate mother, only to find that both her cubs were sitting above him on the tree! As the snarling bear reached his legs, his rifle jammed. Just then, both cubs nose-dived out of the tree onto the ground. The family took off, leaving the terrified hunter clinging to a branch—but alive to tell the tale.

▶Younger grizzlies, called subadults, sometimes look like lanky teenagers. Grizzlies are brown bears whose fur is silver-tipped or grizzled. They have long straight claws for digging. Grizzlies dig huge holes to find mice and marmots. As a bonus, they may come across nuts stashed underground by a squirrel.

A bear mother is loving but strict. She huffs, snarls, and growls her orders. If cubs fail to follow her gestures and vocal commands, they get spanked or cuffed. As they mature, cubs play hard with their siblings. In spite of mom's warnings, they wander away to explore when they get a chance.

By the time cubs become yearlings at nine to 12 months, the 50 to 100-pound animals enter the winter dens with their mothers. By the end of their second summer, these youngsters spend most of their time foraging, following the "maps" made in their memories with their mother's help. Soon they feed and hunt independently. If older cubs hang around, their mother runs them off.

As subadults, young bears rank at the bottom. The largest males are dominant, followed by females with cubs and other adult males. In confrontations, males will sometimes give way to females with cubs. When it's unclear which bear is dominant, they test each other's strength with short fights or threat displays. If subadults survive to become mature males or females, they too will become one of the dominant bears.

The black bear has an unfortunate name. Often this forest dweller isn't black at all. Its fur color sometimes is determined by where it lives and feeds. Studies have shown that west of the Mississippi River, bears feeding on hillsides facing south are more likely to have cinnamon or light fur. In cooler, wetter parts of the eastern U.S. and the Olympic peninsula of Washington state, black bears wear black fur; in the drier Cascade mountains, nearly 60 percent are brown in color.

Another member of this poorly named family is the glacier bear; its fur is bluish-gray. In the Great Bear rainforest of British Columbia, about one out of every ten black bears has a recessive gene. These black bears, called spirit or ghost bears, have white fur.

The most abundant North American species, the black bear eats anything. It prefers sweets and meat, but puts away a much bigger percentage of roots, bulbs, berries, and fruit. With its climbing skills and thick fur to ward off bee stings, the black bear may rob six beehives to get its fill of honey. For meat, this species often goes after frogs, rodents, and fishes, or tackles injured elk, moose, and deer or their young.

A scavenger at heart, a black bear will sample the contents of backpacks, tents, cabins, and henhouses. In the areas of the U.S. and Canada where they are plentiful, it's not unusual to see a bear's rump sticking out of a trash can. Once they develop a taste for human food or domestic animals, black bears are hard to discourage.

Like black bears, members of the once widespread brown bear family can have blue-black, brown, reddish, tan, or blonde fur. In North America, especially among bears in the interior, their fur is often

▶ Black bears aren't always black. They can be brown, tan, or even cinnamon-colored, like this animal drinking water from a stream in Yellowstone National Park.

◄At a salmon run, a grizzly bear may catch up to 15 fish a day. This bear may get neck-deep in water to fish, sometimes pinning salmon against the river rocks on the bottom.

silver-tipped or grizzled—a word which led to them being called "grizzly." Grizzlies, then, are actually brown bears, not a separate species as many people assume. This confusion makes scientists thankful for the grizzly's scientific name, *Ursus arctos*, which is agreed upon by everyone.

In early spring, "brownies," as these bears are also called, look for leftovers. They pounce on fall berries, fruit hidden in the snow, and animals that didn't survive the winter. Although this species gets big—adult grizzlies can weigh 300 to 850 pounds—-most rarely chase healthy deer, elk or moose. Instead, they prey on young or injured animals.

To find more food, brown bears travel up to 75 miles from their den areas to coasts or valleys. There they find small mammals, insects, bird eggs, and soapberries. They feed on shellfish and fish washed ashore. Along the rivers in Siberia, Canada, and Alaska, this species tolerates other bears long enough to share in the month-long summer feasts of spawning salmon.

Kodiak bears are the largest subspecies of brown bears. Living on the remote Kodiak Islands, they are as tall as polar bears but look bigger because their wide heads are simply massive.

In this northern light, the hair of the polar bear looks pink. Its fur isn't pink—or white. Polar bear hairs are clear, hollow, and filled with air. They act as "solar panels," warming the bear's skin.

▶After leaving the birthing den, a polar bear mother often digs a shallow daybed in the snow. Her cubs stay with her two years or more, longer than other bear species. They need time to learn the complex ways of hunting seals and traveling great distances across ice and open water.

As if the whole fur color thing weren't confusing enough, polar bears were once brown bears living in the Siberian forest. Over 100,000 years ago, glaciers stranded some of them. The survivors gradually adapted to arctic weather and life on the ice. They also changed color to blend in better. Now polars are considered a separate species.

Polar bear fur looks white. Surprise: each see-through hair is hollow. In summer, algae sometimes grows inside the hollow hairs, turning polars pale green! The air-filled hairs act as "solar panels," conducting the sun's rays to the bear's black skin. Sunshine plus a thick layer of fat keep the polar bear warm in subzero temperatures.

The stomach of a polar bear can hold 150 pounds of food—and most of it is meat. Although they nibble seaweed and summer berries, they consume far more meat and blubber than other bears. Besides seals, they dig their large sharp teeth into beached whales, walruses, shellfish, eggs, foxes, plus young and injured reindeer, caribou, and musk oxen.

Their hunting success relies on ambush. At a hole in the ice, the bear waits for a ringed seal to come up for air. Grabbing the seal's head with its jaws, the bear jerks

▲ The polar bear eats mostly meat—much more than other bears. At times, it will nibble seaweed or kelp—even diving underwater for it.

▲ There's a reason polar bears hunt ring seals and other seal species. They have the most blubber, the fat that a polar bear needs. A harp seal pup like this one represents a snack—but a predator in the harsh Arctic can't afford to pass up any prey.

▲ Arctic foxes sometimes follow polar bears on the hunt. They feed on the leftovers of the seal meal caught by the polar. If seals are scarce, however, a polar may turn around and dine on a nearby fox instead.

500 pounds of pinniped from the water. When a seal dares to doze on the ice, a polar bear inches toward it. Once it can creep closer, the polar bear takes a giant leap to capture its prey.

Polar bear females breed once every three years so competition over them can get ugly. Males square off to fight; afterwards, the winner has to chase the female across miles of ice to mate her. To give birth, females make snow dens where two to three cubs are born.

Early in life, polar cubs learn to swim and begin to take long trips with their mother. If cubs get too tired swimming in the sea, they ride on mother's back. Along the way, they watch and learn as the female hunts seals for food.

▶A polar bear and her two cubs leap from the ice into a polynya, a Russian word that describes an area of open water surrounded by sea ice. Using their frisbee-sized front paws, polar bears can swim for ten hours and up to 100 miles before taking a break. They also dive. Polars can shut their nostrils and ears before going as deep as 15 feet. Sea ice moves around a great deal. Sometimes polar bears swim underwater from one polynya to another opening in the ice.

As adults, powerful polars can easily swim 100 miles at a time. In summer, the bears sometimes rest on dry land, napping in beds of peat moss. Mostly, however, they swim from one chunk of sea ice to another, roaming across them to hunt.

For centuries, native peoples around the Arctic Circle hunted polars in a sustainable way for meat and hides. When European fur traders arrived in the 17th century, bear numbers began to drop fast. The countries where polar bears were found finally drew up a conservation treaty in 1967. Today's legally protected polar bears live around the North Pole and on sea ice along the shores of Alaska, Canada, Greenland, Norway, and Russia.

Since their home ranges cover thousands of miles, much of it ice, polar bears are uniquely threatened by icecap melt and global warming. Over 20 percent of that ice has vanished since 1979.

Worldwide, a threatened way of life

▶The giant panda of China munches bamboo, almost the only food it eats. It is far more specialized than other bears. Its restricted habitat and diet make it very vulnerable. Human development has destroyed much of the bamboo forest where the panda once wandered.

T he black-and-white body of a giant panda, the world's most high-profile "teddy bear," blends into the snowy shadows of its forest home. Its long coarse fur is dense and woolly underneath. It needs that dandy fur. Pandas have no body fat for warmth and do not hibernate.

The giant panda lives alone, using scent trails and marker trees to find mates and avoid other pandas. It reproduces slowly; its cubs are helpless for six months and stay with the mother for 18 months or more.

Long ago, pandas began to specialize in tree-climbing and bamboo-eating. Each animal spends 15 hours a day gobbling 20 to 40 pounds of bamboo stems and leaves. (Bamboo is low in nutrition, so the panda needs big amounts of it.)

Sad to say, human population and activities have in turn gobbled up the habitat of this shy specialist. To make matters worse, bamboo species have regular periods of die-off. During a 1970s die-off, 138 pandas starved to death.

Once widespread across China and parts of southeast Asia, this most ancient of bears is critically endangered. Somewhere

◀Lesser or red pandas look like raccoons but are close cousins of the giant panda. Shy and gentle, they also live in bamboo forests and eat mainly bamboo. They can live 12 years but are greatly endangered throughout their range, from China to India.

between 1,000 and 2,000 of these appealing animals remain in the wild, half of them living outside of protected reserves.

The Chinese consider giant pandas a national treasure. There's a death penalty for anyone convicted of killing one or smuggling their skins. Despite the risk, poachers and farmers cutting bamboo forests for needed crops reduce panda numbers further. The Chinese success with panda reproduction and cub survival in captivity offers hope. But time is running out for the giant panda in the wild.

Besides wearing ruffs of fur around its head, the moon bear often has chest

▼ South America's only bruin, the spectacled bear makes a daybed in a fig tree, then strips off the fruit. Its cool cloud forest and jungle habitats are disappearing. Surviving bears that live in Bolivia's rainforest reserves are protected.

►Its paws ready to dig for acorns or probe for insects, the chunky moon bear of Asia and eastern Russia may even tackle meatier prey, like deer. Because moon bears also feed on livestock and grain, many are killed as nuisances—or for body parts.

markings shaped like a crescent moon. Also called Asian or Tibetan black bears, this stocky animal builds tree nests to rest in and may hibernate where winters are cold.

Versatile feeders, moon bears eat fruit and carrion in tropical rainforests from Cambodia to China, acorns in Japanese oak forests, insects in the Himalyan foothills, and pine seeds in Russian alpine forests.

Males weigh up to 400 pounds, and can bring down deer and even wild boars. Their fierce tempers and taste for grain and livestock have caused frequent clashes with human beings. As a result, laws to protect them are seldom enforced. About 1,000 are killed annually as nuisance bears. The Chinese view moon bear parts as folk medicine and their paws as gourmet ingredients for soup. Things aren't much better in India, where females are killed so their captured cubs can be trained to dance and ride bicycles.

Spectacled bears, named for the light markings around their eyes, are South America's only bear species. They are the last living examples of short-faced bear species that died out millennia ago. Weighing up to 275 pounds, these adept climbers pick figs and snack on bromeliad plants in the forest canopy. Human development has

►With its long snout, the sloth bear can snorkel up all the termites in sight. A vocal and social creature, it often mingles, gurgles, and yelps with other sloth bears.

taken away much of their range, from lowland jungle to cool cloud forest.

Spectacled bears are targets for their meat and fat, thought of as a medicine for rheumatism. Although still looked at as threats to crops and cattle, most spectacled bears live in 56 protected areas, including some of Bolivia's richest jungles.

Another food specialist, the sloth bear has grown a flexible, piglike snout and lost its front teeth in the bargain, all the better to slurp up termites and ants. Sloth bears also eat fruit, roots, and dead critters they run across. In the spring, they compete with human beings over the waxy blooms of the Mohwa tree. The bear eats the creamy flowers; the townspeople, however, prefer to collect them to make an alcoholic drink.

This animal is unusually social for a bear, huffing and squeaking with others. A medium-sized animal, it has silky black fur to which its cubs cling like baby possums. Sloth bears live in thorn forests and humid jungles from India to Sri Lanka. Drastic cutting of these forests has caused a huge drop in their numbers, but efforts to protect tiger habitat in India may help this homely little bear survive.

The small sun bear gets its nickname from the yellow splash of color it often wears on its chest. A little-known species, it gets more endangered as Southeast Asia rainforests disappear.

A neat, doglike animal, the sun bear has short black fur, a light muzzle, and one of the longest tongues you've ever seen. It shinnies up trees like a lineman climbing a telephone pole. Besides slurping insects and going deep into hives for honey, this 60 to 150-pound bear lives on snails, earthworms, fruit, and lizards. It also has heavy canines, perhaps developed to defend itself from area leopards, snakes, and tigers.

◄A more doglike bear, the sun bear has short hair and a very long tongue—the better to lap up earthworms and honey. It lives in southeast Asia, where snakes and tigers prowl. The sun bear probably developed those big canine teeth to defend itself.

Saving teddy

Bear numbers plummeted in the 20th century. All eight species remain endangered or threatened. As human populations soar, using up land and natural resources, the wilderness that bears need disappears more each day.

As cubs and young adults in the wild, bears are vulnerable. Without home ranges yet, they have to keep out of the way of more dominant bears. Once they reach five years or so, bears have few natural enemies. In North America, wolves are a threat and so are hunters with dogs. In Asia and India, tigers and snakes are the only foes. In the

◄ Being up a tree is nothing new for a black bear cub. It is taught by its mother to climb at signs of danger. If the cub disobeys, mom will cuff it—or spank it. Mother bears often make daybeds for their cubs at the foot of tall trees.

►Human visitors who want to eavesdrop on grizzlies at McNeil River and other prime bear-watching sites in Alaska and Canada must learn safety rules. They must keep 50 yards away from animals, make noise as they walk through the forest, and yield right of way to the animals.

Arctic, sometimes very young, old, or injured polar bears get preyed upon by killer whales and bull walruses.

The greatest danger of all to bears comes from human predators.

It wasn't always like this. Stone Age hunters and tribal cultures in North America viewed the bear with respect and made it part of their mythology. To many, the bear served as a messenger between the spirit world and theirs.

By the time of the Roman Empire, so many bears were slaughtered in savage displays that bear populations in North Africa were completely wiped out. Later cultures, like the English and other Europeans, were equally cruel with their bear-baiting events and cub captures for circus work. Settlers in Canada and the U.S. thought of bears as varmints, then as sources of food and furs. As people moved westward, prime habitat vanished and the animals retreated to more remote areas.

In 1902, U.S. President Teddy Roosevelt refused to shoot a black bear chained to a tree. By making this widely publicized gesture and by establishing the first national parks, environmentalist Roosevelt helped Americans see bears and wilderness in a different light. Toys called "teddy bears" were made to honor the event; they remain a favorite icon of popular culture, more than a century later.

Although most species have legal protection on paper, bears are threatened by global warming, pollution, and poachers. As the world warms and the Arctic sea ice melts away beneath polar bear feet, their populations face starvation—even extinction. Arctic oil drilling also increases

the possibility of oil spills and harm to bears.

Poachers still kill bears of every species. The internet has made it easy to sell bear body parts worldwide as trophies, gourmet food items, and medicinal ingredients. The trade in bile from wild black bears and grizzlies is especially damaging. In China, so-called "bear farms" insert large drain tubes into the abdomens of caged bears, causing great suffering. Bear bile has medicinal value but it can be replicated in the lab without using bears.

In many countries, bears are still looked at as nuisances and killed illegally. Conflicts between human populations and bears continue. Campers, hikers, and visitors who come to parks such as Yellowstone often fail to respect bears' need for personal space. Some even put themselves and their children in jeopardy, trying to get close for photographs or feeding the animals. Each year tragedies occur and a handful of people

◄ In late fall, hundreds of polar bears gather along the coast of Hudson Bay near the Canadian town of Churchill. Male bears are waiting for the sea to freeze over so they can hunt seals. Female polars are there to make dens on land where cubs will be born. In tundra buggies like this one, visitors can see and photograph these awesome animals, which are three times the size of a lion.

get mauled or killed. Most often, however, these situations end up badly for the bear. Once hooked on garbage or handouts, a bear spells trouble. Sometimes the bear can be relocated. But repeat offenders, often females pushed out of their home ranges, must be destroyed.

What can be done to save the dwindling remnants of these ancient species?

The biggest priority is the preservation of wilderness habitat—especially in Alaska and Canada, the last great lands for three species of these animals. To help, join global organizations like the Natural Resources Defense Council (NRDC); they spearheaded the campaign to win government protection for Canada's Great Bear rainforest, among other victories.

More parks, reserves, and legal protections are needed, especially for pandas and other bears teetering on the brink of extinction. More attention needs to be paid to the illegal trafficking in bear parts—and surer punishment for those who make such ugly acts their business.

In our lives, bears should be more than cartoon characters or "poster animals" for fire prevention. As one of earth's most charismatic mammals, they are key figures in the delicate dance between all living things in the food chain. Whether real bears ever cross your path or not, their pawprints should keep on circling the earth and snow of our planet. Their clawmarks on trees should continue to send messages in a scent language we cannot decipher.

They belong here, just as we do. And just as rightly.

▼ A polar bear leaves big paw prints in the Arctic snow. These graceful predators move equally well on ice, thanks to small bumps on their feet that keep them from slipping.

Secrets of bears

- Getting ready for their winter's nap, grizzly bears eat up to 20,000 calories a day and put on six to ten inches of fat.

- Bear cubs have daily lessons. For two years, their mother teaches them a "map" of their home range, showing them where to harvest berries, hunt insects, fish for salmon, and make dens.

- When brown bears have silver-tipped fur, they're called grizzlies—but they are still brown bears. Black bears are poorly named, too. They often have brown, cinnamon, or blondish fur.

- A polar bear looks white—but its hollow hairs are see-through, not pigmented. In summer, a polar bear might even look pale green because of plant algae growing inside each hair.

- Bears that hibernate need fatty foods. Salmon is one. Nuts are another. So are insects like moths! When they can get them, bears gobble thousands of moths.

- How does hibernation work? The bear slows down its heart rate and burns 25% of its stored fat to survive. Hibernation can last from two to seven months.

- A bear's nose is a real wonder. Inside its mouth it has special nerve endings that help the nose sniff even better. Upwind, a bear can smell food—or you—over a mile away.

- Most of the world's grizzlies live within 100 miles of the Pacific ocean. Why? To be near the rivers where salmon, their favorite fatty food, spawns each year.

- Cubs make a sweet humming sound as they nurse. Sometimes their den is crowded. A mother bear in good condition can have up to five cubs in a litter.

- Over time, the giant panda got so specialized that it eats only bamboo. Sometimes a big part of its food supply flowers and dies, leaving the panda to starve.

- Sloth bears vacuum up termites. South American spectacled bears snack on figs and bromeliad plants. The sun bear likes honey and fruit but won't turn down earthworms or lizards.

◄ Human beings can learn to co-exist with bears, but it takes effort and good will. Fishermen and bears often compete for salmon—but unlike wild bruins, human beings are able to change jobs and choose other foods.

Glossary

Bear bile. Liquid secreted by a bear's gall bladder. It helps digest fats in a bear's food. Bear bile is in high demand for traditional Chinese medicine. To obtain it, moon bears and other species are killed illegally or kept in abusive conditions.

Bluff charge. When bears want to threaten instead of fight, they rush at another bear (or a human being) in a pretend attack, called a bluff charge.

Canines. The four sharp, pointed teeth in the front of a bear's mouth. Dogs, the original canines, also have canine teeth.

Denning. The yearly actions of certain bear species. They make dens or lairs in which to hibernate and/or give birth to cubs.

Die-off. The sudden but natural death of a large number of plants or animals. After blooming, some bamboo species go through a die-off, leaving giant pandas without food.

Dominance hierarchy. Pecking order that bears establish among themselves to reduce aggression. Older, larger bears are dominant.

Forage. To hunt, gather, and eat plant and animal foods.

Global warming. Well-established theory that the earth is warming rapidly due to the burning of fossil fuel and other human activities.

Hibernation. A state of greatly reduced activity. To hibernate, bears lower their body temperatures and heart-rates. The word comes from the Latin for winter but some bears hibernate much longer.

Incisors. A bear's front teeth, located in front of the canine teeth.

Marking tree. Special trees that are marked with the scent, claw marks, and hair of many bears. These signs act as messages for other bears that sniff them.

Molars. Flat teeth, found at the back of a bear's mouth and adapted for grinding plants.

Omnivore. An animal, such as a bear, that eats a wide variety of plant and animal foods. Human beings are also omnivores.

Poacher. A human hunter that captures or kills illegal prey, such as endangered bears. Poachers sell bear body parts for food or medicine and live cubs as pets.

Scavenger. Animal that eats dead organic matter like garbage or the kill brought down by another animal. If hungry, bears and many other creatures will scavenge.

Subadult. A bear that no longer is nursed by its mother but is not fully grown. It takes five years or more for a bear to reach maturity.

►Bears, especially black bears, are natural scavengers. Once they get hooked on garbage and handouts, they lose their fear of human beings. Long ago, bears were deliberately fed garbage to amuse human audiences in places like Yellowstone. Today, park rangers teach visitors about the dangers of feeding bears.

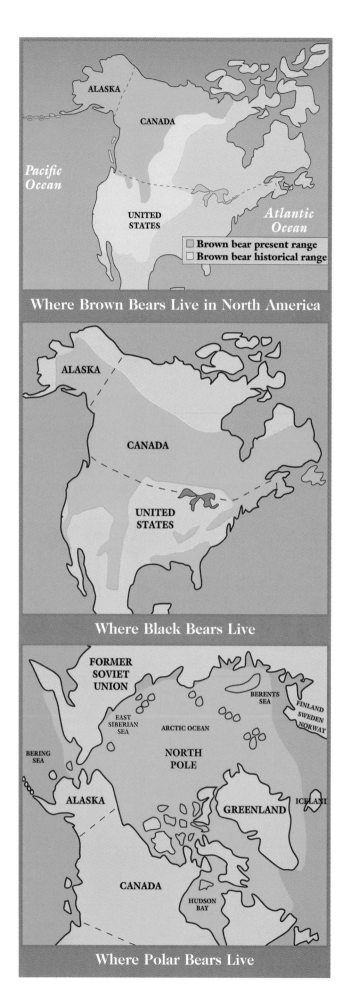

Where Brown Bears Live in North America

☐ Brown bear present range
☐ Brown bear historical range

Pacific Ocean

Atlantic Ocean

ALASKA

CANADA

UNITED STATES

Where Black Bears Live

ALASKA

CANADA

UNITED STATES

Where Polar Bears Live

FORMER SOVIET UNION

EAST SIBERIAN SEA

BERING SEA

ALASKA

ARCTIC OCEAN

NORTH POLE

BERENTS SEA

FINLAND SWEDEN NORWAY

GREENLAND

ICELAND

CANADA

HUDSON BAY

About the author

Nature writer Joni Hunt has written other books in this series, including *A Shimmer of Butterflies* and *A Chorus of Frogs.*

Photographers

The 32 storytelling photos by Jeff Foott, principal photographer, come from decades of patient pursuit of his furry subjects. A noted cinematographer, Jeff's nature films for public televison and other venues have won many awards. Eleven images from eight other wildlife photographers round out the book: Tom Bean/DRK Photo, p. 20; John Cancalosi/DRK Photo, p. 35; J.M. Labat/Jacana/Photo Researchers, p. 37; Wayne Lankinen/DRK Photo, p. 40; Wayne Lynch/DRK Photo, p. 18; Tom McHugh/Photo Researchers, pp 36, 38; Mark D. Phillips/Photo Researchers, p. 39; Art Wolfe, front cover, pp 33, 34.

Special thanks

Brian Cahill, ranger at Redwoods State Park, California
Dr. Charles Jonkel, Great Bear Foundation
Dr. Richard Murphy, Ocean Futures Society

Where to see bears

- **In captivity:** most of the zoos worldwide display at least one species. Giant pandas are on longterm loan to zoos in San Diego, California; Washington D.C.; Atlanta, Georgia; and Memphis, Tennessee. Zoos in Germany, Austria, Mexico, Japan, and Thailand also have a few but the majority of captive or zoo-bred pandas are in Chinese zoos and research centers.
- **In the wild:** remember that bears get dangerous if they feel threatened. Be cautious and respect "bear etiquette." Never feed, tease, get too close, or run away from wild bears.
- Likely places to spot black bears, brown bears or grizzlies in North America include Banff National Park and Lake Louise, Alberta, Canada; Katmai NP, Denali NP and Denali State Park in Alaska; Glacier NP in Montana and Canada; Great Smoky Mountains NP in Tennessee and North Carolina; Mt. Everstoke NP, British Columbia, Canada; Waterton NP, Alberta, Canada; Yellowstone NP in Wyoming; and Yosemite NP in California.
- McNeil River State Game Sanctuary, SW Alaska. Photographers' heaven, perhaps the world's best place to view bear interactions as they fish for salmon. Adjacent to Katmai NP. Entry restricted; permits chosen by lottery and visits accompanied by resident biologists.
- Katmai National Park, Alaska. Good viewing from an elevated platform at Brooks Falls. The park has a bear population in the hundreds.
- Churchill, on Hudson Bay in Manitoba, Canada. October and November, polar bear viewing from tundra buggies and fascinating programs through the Churchill Northern Studies Centre.
- Admiralty Island National Monument, Alaska. Best place near Juneau for grizzly viewing at Pack Creek.
- Fish Creek Wildlife Observation Site, near Hyder, Alaska. Platform viewing at Bear Creek of both black bears and grizzlies. Charter boats also go to Kodiak and other islands where there are concentrated numbers of bears.

Helping organizations & good websites

- Earthwatch Institute, 3 Clock Tower Place, #100, Maynard MA 01754. On this excellent website, kids can learn about ongoing field work to save bear species, their habitats, and wildlife corridors for animals between fragments of wilderness. Students can take part in some field expeditions and challenge projects; teachers can use the Classroom Earth series for middle and high school units. (www.earthwatch.org)
- Churchill Northern Studies Centre, PO Box 610, Manitoba, Canada R0B 0E0. Polar bear courses, ProjectWild conservation program for educators, and a variety of 5-day learning vacations. Good links to other resources. (www.churchillmb.net/cnsc/)
- Polar Bears International, PO Box 66142, Baton Rouge LA 70896. Videos, photo gallery. Good arctic map, interesting educational site. (www.polarbearsalive.org)
- Great Bear Foundation, PO Box 9383, Missoula MT 59807. A global group, dedicated to preserving all eight bear species. Offers field programs for kids six and up. (www.greatbear.org)
- International Association for Bear Research and Management. A nonprofit bear conservation group, mostly for professionals in the field. Excellent fact sheets on the eight bear species. (www.bearbiology.com)
- Natural Resources Defense Council (NRDC), 40 West 20th St, New York NY 10011. One of the most effective groups around has a superb website: "Make Waves" kid action programs, virtual marches, online movies, and great summaries on hot-button environmental issues. (www.nrdc.org)

To learn more

Recommended books:
- Bauer, Erwin and Peggy. *Bears of Alaska*. (Sasquatch Books 2002).
- Craighead, Lance. *Bears of the World*. (Voyageur Press 2000).
- Fergus, Charles. *Bears*. (Wild Guide series, Stackpole Press 2005).

Magazines:
- "A Galling Situation." By Barry Estabrook. *Wildlife Conservation* magazine, August 2006, pp 26 – 31. Details about the dark side of the bear bile market.
- "Power Lunch." By Jeff Fair. *Audubon* magazine, July-August 2006, pp 50 – 56.
- "Panda, Inc." by Lynne Warren. *National Geographic*, July 2006, pp 42 – 59. Informative update on the world status of pandas, captive, zoo born, and wild; beguiling photos.

Videos, DVDs, and films:
- "The Great Bears." Discovery Channel/BBC 1992. VHS format, 1 hour.
- "The Grizzlies." National Geographic 1992. VHS format, 1 hour. Spectacular footage, lucid explanation of the brown bear/grizzly connection.
- "Bears." IMAX 2001. DVD format, 85 minutes. Great overview of polar, black bear, and other species.
- "Last Stand of the Great Bear." National Geographic 2004. DVD format, 1 hour.
- "China—the Panda Adventure." IMAX 2001 drama. 49 minutes.
- "Loaded for Polar Bears." Westlake 2004. DVD format, 1 hour.

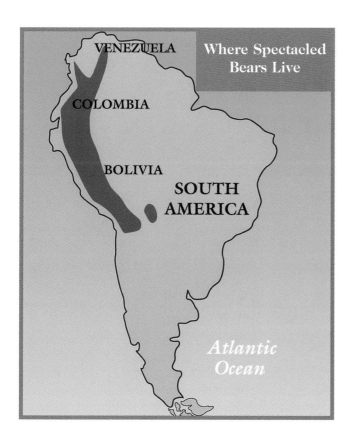

Where Spectacled Bears Live

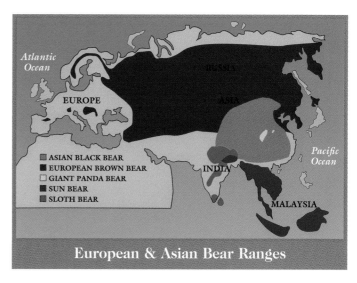

European & Asian Bear Ranges

Index

Photographs are numbered in **boldface** and follow the print references after **PP** (photo page).